Encyclopædia Britannica

Fascinating Facts

Nature

PUBLICATIONS INTERNATIONAL, LTD.

Encyclopædia Britannica, Inc.
310 South Michigan Ave.
Chicago, IL 60604

Printed and bound in USA.

8 7 6 5 4 3 2

ISBN: 1-56717-322-9

SERIES PICTURE CREDITS:

Keeping Track of Weather

Weather is the state of our atmosphere. These conditions may change from day to day or even from hour to hour, and they include clouds, rain, wind, cold, heat, or even sunshine or snow.

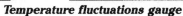
Temperature fluctuations gauge

What's the Weather Like?

Knowing what the weather will be does more than help us decide what clothes to wear or whether or not to bring an umbrella with us. Farmers need to know the weather in order to plan when they will plant seeds in the ground and when they will harvest their crops. Power plants can get ready to supply heat in case it gets unusually cold. People can get buildings ready or can get themselves to safety if they know a huge storm is coming. And ship captains and pilots can steer away from storms or other problems if they know about them ahead of time.

Climates vs. Weather

Climate is the average effect of weather—what it is like over a long period of time. Even though it might be rainy today, for example, an area's climate might be called dry because it only has about fifteen rainy days each year.

Dew drops form on the morning grass.

Up in the Clouds

Clouds are made of millions of drops of water or ice, all floating together in the air. Clouds form when air is cooled and the water in it begins to condense into droplets. If this happens on the ground, dew—the drops of water you see on the grass in the morning—forms. If it happens up in the atmosphere, clouds form as the air rises higher and higher into the sky.

Cloudy Days, Sunny Days

Some parts of the world have more clouds than others. The air over deserts, for example, is so dry that clouds do not form very often. Areas around oceans and seas have a lot of moisture in the air. As a result, there are a lot more clouds in these locations.

Different Kinds of Clouds

Scientists have found ten types of clouds that they have named. The three that we see most often are: *cirrus* clouds (the feathery clouds that float very high up in the sky); *cumulus* clouds (the puffy clouds that are flat at the bottom and rounded on top); and *stratus* clouds (layered clouds that seem to hang like a gray blanket over the earth).

It Sure Looks Like Rain

Rain is caused by water vapor (visible moisture) in the air. Air always contains a certain amount of moisture. If that air cools, it *condenses,* or forms into water. At first, droplets are very small. They slowly get bigger until they are too heavy to stay up in the air. Then, these drops fall to earth as rain.

Caught in the Rain

"Cloudburst" is a name that we give to a sudden, hard rainstorm. You probably have seen this kind of rain—it seems to suddenly just pour down from the heavens.

Different Sizes of Raindrops

The average raindrop is about $^1/_{100}$ of an inch ($^1/_2$ mm) around. In the heavy showers of the tropics, however, they can be much, much larger—up to $^1/_{50}$ to $^1/_{12}$ of an inch (1 to 3 mm) across.

Rain or No Rain? ▲

The rainiest place in the world is probably in Assam, in northern India. An average of 425 inches (10,820 mm) of rain falls there each year. The driest place is the Atacama Desert in northern Chile. No rain has fallen there for hundreds of years.

White Flakes of Snow

Snow is caused by the same conditions as rain. The difference is simply a matter of how cold it is in the air when the water vapor condenses. When it is cold enough, the vapor changes directly into ice crystals. At fairly low temperatures, the crystals stay separate and float in the air as glittering specks. Once the temperature goes below the freezing point (32°F or 0°C), the ice crystals join together into white flakes we call snow.

Keeping the Ground Warm with Snow ▼

Strangely enough, a layer of snow can help keep the ground warm enough to stop it from freezing. There is a great amount of air in the midst of all those crystals of ice that make up a snowflake. Since air is one of the best non-conductors of heat and cold, a covering of snow actually acts like a blanket on the ground. It keeps in the warmth that built up in the ground over the summer and fall. It also keeps out much of the cold that comes from the air above. Although some of the top layers of soil may freeze, the rest of the ground will usually be much warmer.

Beautiful Snowflakes

The size and shape of a snowflake depend on the temperature outside and on the amount of water in the flake itself. This tends to make each snowflake unique. It is also true that all snowflakes are basically *hexagons*, shapes with six sides.

Blowing Blizzards ▶

Years ago, the term "blizzard" was used only for the extremely cold snowstorms that blew across the Great Plains of North America. Now, we use the term a lot more loosely. To most of us, a blizzard is simply an extremely big snowstorm that brings with it high winds and blowing snow.

Hail from the Sky ▲

Hail is made up of little balls of ice up to 4 inches (10 cm) big. Hailstones are formed in thunderclouds. When a strong draft of air carries water droplets to the top of a thundercloud, they freeze and turn into tiny balls of ice. These small balls of ice then fall to the lower part of the cloud where more water droplets cling to them and freeze around them. If these frozen balls of ice meet more updrafts of air, they can be carried up and down several times. Eventually, they collect enough layers that they fall out of a cloud and reach the earth as hail.

Damaging Hailstones

Most of the time, hailstones are so small that they cannot harm people. But, they often damage farmers' crops, beating down wheat, cotton, or corn and damaging trees. When hailstones are quite large—as big as a tennis ball—they can be very dangerous. Reports have been heard of chickens, dogs, and even cows being injured or killed by hailstones.

The Force of Tornadoes

Tornadoes have been known to pick up just about anything in their swirling, twisting winds. Trees, automobiles, and even heavily loaded freight trains have all been lifted up by these fierce storms.

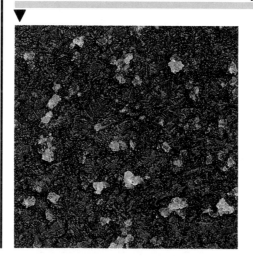

A Sheet of Sleet

Sleet is smaller-sized hail. It is made up of tiny globes of ice, usually no more than $1/5$ inch (5 mm) in diameter. It forms when raindrops or partially melted snowflakes freeze.

Snow Clouds ◄

Although precipitation (rain, sleet, hail, and snow) can form in many different kinds of clouds, snow, hail, and sleet seem to come most often from cumulus clouds—those puffy clouds with round tops and flat bottoms.

North vs. South

North of the equator, in the Northern Hemisphere, cyclone winds turn counterclockwise. In the Southern Hemisphere, however, they turn in exactly the opposite way—clockwise.

Spiraling Storms

Both cyclones and tornadoes are storms made up of spiraling, twisting winds. Tornadoes, though, are usually more violent. Cyclones can form at any time, and they often bring with them snow, rain, or hail. Tornadoes usually (although not always) start when thunderstorms are forming, and they do not always bring precipitation with them.

Cyclones leave devastation in their paths.

Where Most Cyclones Occur ▬

Cyclones have been known to form everywhere on earth except around the equator. However, they are more common in the middle latitudes of both hemispheres— along the American Middle West, for example, and through the middle of South America and Australia.

Twisting Tornadoes ▬

Tornadoes move across land at up to 40 miles (64 km) per hour, but their winds move at far greater speeds. A typical tornado has winds moving at up to 300 miles (480 km) per hour. The winds at the center of some tornadoes have been measured to be twisting around at almost 500 miles (800 km) an hour.

Tornadoes of the Seas

For centuries, sailors have made reports about twisting storms called "waterspouts." Most waterspouts are tornadoes that have moved over a lake or ocean and draw water up into the air. A slower and less severe type of waterspout is caused by a warm air pocket drawing the tip of a rain cloud down to a body of water.

Tropical Storms Called Hurricanes

Hurricanes are violent tropical storms that start up in areas of unstable wind conditions and a large area of water with warm temperatures (80°F; 27°C). Because of the way the earth turns, the winds end up traveling in a spiral. (Like cyclones and tornadoes, hurricanes in the Northern Hemisphere have winds traveling counter-clockwise; in the Southern Hemisphere, they travel clockwise. A hurricane is like a giant wheel lying on its side, with winds up to 100 miles per hour (160 kph) spinning around a calm center.

The Salt of the Ocean

The ocean is salty because rivers have been carrying pieces of soil and rock into the oceans of the world for millions of years. Some of these pieces sink to the bottom of the ocean and become part of the sediment at the bottom of the sea. Some particles end up being dissolved in the ocean. Salt is the most common natural substance dissolved in this way.

Freezing Salty Water

As water becomes more and more salty, it takes colder and colder temperatures to freeze it. As a result, the average temperature in the ocean is usually too high to ever really freeze the water. Even when the surface does freeze, as it does at the North Pole, the depths beneath it do not. At the North Pole, for example, there is only about 50 feet (15 m) of ice.

More and More Salt

Our oceans are actually getting saltier every year because water evaporates more quickly than is added by rain, while dissolved salt stays there forever.

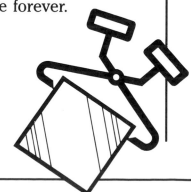

Watching the Waves

Waves form when wind blows over the water from the same direction for several hours. The longer the wind blows in that direction, the bigger and longer-lasting the waves will be. These waves even continue after the wind dies down, although they get weaker and weaker. That's one of the reasons why the water is so calm in some areas—it is far from the "prevailing winds" (the direction from which wind usually comes).

A Warm-water Current

The Gulf Stream is an ocean current that runs from the Gulf of Mexico all the way to the Arctic Ocean. Helped by the wind, it brings warm water into the Atlantic and carries it northward.

From Warm to Cold

There are several currents in the Atlantic. In fact, the Gulf Stream flows very close to one of the other currents, the Labrador Current. Near Newfoundland, on Canada's eastern coast the warm Gulf Stream and icy cold Labrador Currents are actually just a few yards apart. The waters of the two currents never mingle together—temperatures may vary tremendously between the two areas just a few yards apart.

High Tide, Low Tide

Tides are movements of the oceans' water that are caused by the moon's and sun's gravity. For part of a day, each section of a seacoast has a high tide when the water rises high up on the beach and a low tide when the water falls back. Since the moon and the earth rotate around each other, the water on the side of the earth away from the moon is constantly being thrown outward, creating a bulge of water on that side of the earth. On the side of the earth facing the moon, there is another bulge since the pull of the moon is strongest here. The earth spins on its axis once every 24 hours—any place on earth passes through a region of high water twice a day.

Powerful Ocean Currents

Some currents are caused by winds, which blow across the ocean in the same direction all year long. As these winds blow, they move the surface of the sea with them, carrying along particles of water. Some currents, like the Gulf Stream in the North Atlantic, are surface currents. Others run deep below the surface of the sea. These currents are caused by the earth's rotation, moving the water at an angle of about 90° to the direction of the prevailing wind.

Making Coral

Coral comes from the skeletons of dead sea animals, or polyps, which contain a hard skeleton of calcium carbonate. The skeletons join and link together to form fans, reefs, and even whole islands. Meanwhile, other living polyps move in among the skeletons where they eventually die, keeping the reef or island growing layer by layer.

Cold-water Coral

Most of us think of coral as something found only in the warm waters of the Pacific or the Caribbean. It is true that coral does much better in water above 70°F (21°C). However, it does grow in other places—even in the North Atlantic and the icy fjords of Norway.

Different Names for Different Shapes

Coral polyps often live together in colonies. They assume a distinctive shape, after which their coral is named. "Brain coral," "stag horn coral," and "mushroom coral" are just a few of the many different kinds of coral that can be found in the sea.

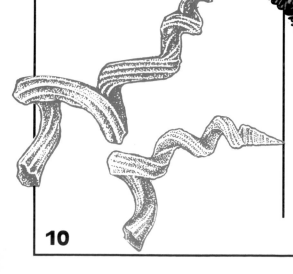

Coral Jewelry

For thousands of years, the red coral found in the Mediterranean has been treated as a precious stone. Ancient Romans even believed that it could keep diseases away from children. Today, we use red coral for jewelry, a function that regular reef coral can't provide.

Great Barrier Reef

Building a Reef

A reef is the result of millions of years of polyp skeletons piled layer upon layer. The coral rock in a reef is fairly soft, so many sea creatures find shelter in its twists, turns, and folds. The Great Barrier Reef off the northeastern coast of Australia is one of the largest and best-known reefs in the world.

Brightly colored reef fish make their homes on coral.

All Reefs are not Alike

There are three basic kinds of reefs. *Fringing* reefs surround islands and continents, without leaving room for water between the land and the sea. *Barrier* reefs are like fringing reefs except that they are much farther away from the land. There is often a channel wide and deep enough to allow ocean-going ships to pass between the reef and the land. The third kind of reef is an *atoll,* which is shaped like a ring or horseshoe.

Fascinating Reef Creatures

Reefs are full of unusual creatures. Among the best known are brightly colored reef fish. These fish find an excellent home in reefs because the coral gives them places to hide from larger fish. Many kinds of shellfish also make their homes in reefs, including starfish, shrimp, and crabs. One of these shellfish, the crown-of-thorns starfish, actually feeds on coral polyps, and is responsible for destroying huge sections of Australia's Great Barrier Reef. Another reef-dweller is the great moray eel, a deadly creature that uses needlelike teeth to tear apart almost anything.

Volcanic Reefs ▲

Atolls, unlike other reefs, are usually found in the open ocean. They begin as ordinary coral reefs that surround, or fringe, an island formed by a volcano. As these island volcanos sink very slowly into the sea, the coral grows upward very quickly in order to get to the light of the sun. In time, the volcano disappears completely and all that is left is a ring surrounding an empty center.

Record-breaking Eruption

The biggest volcanic explosion in the recent past took place on Rakata, an island in Indonesia. In 1883, there were several earthquakes and small eruptions. A series of huge explosions followed, destroying most of Krakatoa, a volcano on the island, and the island itself. The noise of the blast could be heard 3,000 miles (5,000 km) away. Over 36,000 people were drowned by the waves set off by the eruption of this volcano.

Lakes of Water ▲

A lake is a large sheet of water surrounded by land. The water is in a basin, or hollow, in the surface of the earth. A rim around the basin keeps the water from flowing out.

Dying Lakes

From the moment they are formed, lakes start to "die." The streams and rivers that flow from a lake, for example, grow deeper and deeper as they cut into the soil and rock they run through. As a result, more and more water fills them—and runs out of the lake. Streams flowing into a lake also bring in mud and pebbles that gradually fill in the lake itself. More recently, pollution of the air and water has added another factor—algae, weeds, and acid rain are clogging our lakes.

Islands Formed from Volcanoes

Many volcanoes are located on ridges in the middle of the ocean or along the edges of the world's oceans. The Hawaiian Islands, for example, are volcanic islands located on a ridge in the Pacific; Iceland is another volcanic island located in the North Atlantic. Elsewhere, the Aleutian Islands are formed from a chain of volcanoes, while the Andes Mountains of South America began as volcanoes along the coast.

How Lakes are Made

Lakes are formed in many different ways. Many lakes were formed during the Ice Age, when glaciers carved great hollows in the earth's surface. As the glaciers moved rocks and blocked ancient rivers, dams were created that turned the areas behind them into lakes. Most of the world's biggest lakes were formed by movements in the earth's crust. Earthquakes, cracks, and collapses all formed lakes in their own ways. Volcanoes have also formed many lakes, as the hollow at the center of a dead volcano slowly fills with water.

A Lake by any Other Name...

There are many interesting lakes in the world. One of them, the Dead Sea, is not even called a lake at all. Another sea that is really a lake is the Caspian Sea in Central Asia. The deepest lake in the world is Lake Baikal, which is almost 5,000 feet (1,525 m) deep.

The Story of Salty Rivers

Some rivers are actually salty because of the action of tides, which draws the sea's saltwater up into the river. They also get salty in dry, hot weather when the fresh water of a river evaporates and leaves salt behind.

Disappearing Water

Water disappears in three main ways. Some of it *evaporates*, meaning that as it gets warmed by the sun, it turns to vapor and is carried off by the wind. Some gathers together to form streams. The rest sinks into the soil and then reappears through springs and flows into streams, rivers, and lakes.

River Water Travelers

Rivers do not just carry water; they also carry soil and rock. The muddy color of many rivers comes from the particles of clay that are carried along by the flowing water. All of these particles of dirt and rock, along with the water that carries them, slowly wear away the river bed. As a result, even more rock and soil are carried by the river. Although it takes a long time, this can create very deep cuts in the earth. In fact, the Grand Canyon was formed in this way.

Little Streams, Bigger Rivers

Rivers are formed when streams join to form larger streams, these larger streams join together to form still larger streams, and so on. Rivers then carry water along until they deposit them in other rivers, the ocean, or the sea.

Cavernous Caves

Caves are deep hollow spaces that are found in the rocky sides of hills or cliffs. Very large caves are sometimes called caverns.

How a Cave is Made

Caves near seaside cliffs are often made by waves bashing against the rocks. Other caves are formed as hard rocks rub against softer rocks. Most caves away from the shore, however, are formed by underground streams and rivers that slowly wear away layers of soft rock.

Interior Wonders

Stalactites and stalagmites are formed by mineral deposits in a cave. *Stalactites* hang down from the ceiling of a cave; *stalagmites* grow up from the cave's floor. They grow slowly, as calcite from rocks outside the cave passes into the cave. As water comes into the cave, it is deposited very slowly, particle by particle, until the long form of stalactites or stalagmites is formed. This takes a long time—sometimes hundreds of years—but the results are wonderful to see.

A Very Big Cave

Mammoth Cave, in Kentucky, is one of the largest and most spectacular caves in the world. The land above it takes up an area almost 9 miles (15 km) wide, and it contains more than 155 miles (250 km) of tunnels and hallways.

The Story of Cavemen

There really were cavemen thousands of years ago. Scientists have found hundreds of caves in which people lived. Not all prehistoric people were cave dwellers, but many of them did take shelter in the deep, warm caves of Europe and Asia.

Cave Inhabitants

Deep inside Mammoth Cave are some of the world's most unusual creatures. Eyeless, blind fish swim in the cave's streams and rivers. Blind grasshoppers, beetles, rats, and huge numbers of large bats also live in the cave.

Moving Glaciers

A glacier is a mass of ice moving along the surface of the earth. Some glaciers move only an inch or two each year, while others may move as much as several hundred yards (or meters) in a single year.

Glaciers Around the World

Glaciers are found just about anywhere there is a lot of snow. You can find them at the North and South Poles, in high mountain areas, and in the frozen Arctic regions. It's also why you find glaciers along the equator in Africa—they are so high up in the mountains that it is freezing all year round.

Glacier Power

Glaciers changed the face of the earth by moving slowly along the surface carrying along rocks, dirt, and even giant boulders. All of these scrape the ground beneath and around the glacier, slowly cutting away the surface to form valleys, hollows, and other shapes. Glaciers often just drop off some of this material, making hills and other land formations.

From Glaciers to Icebergs

Glaciers begin to melt whenever they reach the *snow line,* the point above which snow stays in summer. However, some glaciers are so big that they reach all the way past the snow line to the sea. In cold regions, like the Arctic and Greenland, glaciers often reach the sea, where huge blocks of ice often break and drift off as icebergs.

Grouping Mountains

Most mountains are found in groups called "chains," "ranges," or "massifs." The highest mountains of all are found in two long lines, one circling the Pacific Ocean and the other stretching from Spain to the East Indies. Most of these were formed by the action of rivers and glaciers on large portions of the earth that have been pushed up by action in the earth's interior.

Mountain Measurements

According to most scientists, a mass of rock must be at least 1,640 feet (500 m) high in order to be considered a mountain. Anything smaller than that is just a hill.

Mountain Greats

The highest mountains in the world are the Himalayas, in northern India and Tibet, and the Andes, in South America. Each of these great mountain ranges encircles a high flat plateau over 13,000 feet (4,000 m) in the air.

Rocky Mountains

Frost, running water, and glaciers give mountains their rocky appearance. These elements cut and scrape away at the surface, creating peaks, gorges, cuts, and valleys. Without this, mountains would be just round- or flat-topped masses of soil.

Down in the Valley

Valleys are natural troughs or hollows in the surface of the earth. At the bottom of a valley is its floor, a flat surface that slopes off in one direction or another. The sides, called slopes, are then angled up.

Not a Real Valley ▲

Death Valley, like the Great Valley of California, was not formed in the ways valleys usually are and is not a valley at all. It was formed when a long, narrow section of the earth's crust sank below the surrounding area.

Making a Valley ▲

Most valleys were formed by streams, rivers, and floodwaters running over them. The running water carries rocks and soil along with it, slowly cutting into the surface of the earth until the trench of the valley is formed. Other valleys have been created by the movement of glaciers as they scraped their way along the earth.

The Grandest Canyon of All ▼

A canyon is nothing more than a valley with extremely steep sides. One of the most famous canyons is the Grand Canyon, in Arizona. It is over a mile (1.6 km) deep in many spots and ranges from 2 to 18 miles (3 to 29 km) across.

It's Worth Its Weight in Gold ▲

Gold is valuable because it is a very stable substance in terms of its chemistry and is not affected very much by weather, air, or even water. Gold lasts a very long time and doesn't change much over the years. Gold is also very scarce. If you lumped together all of the gold produced and used in history so far, you would end up with a block the size of a large house. With only a little bit of gold in the world, it's no wonder that people pay a high price for it.

There is Nothing Like Gold ▶

Gold is a heavy metal that is often found embedded in rock in "veins." It must be separated from the rock by breaking it into tiny pieces so that it can be processed. Once this process is completed, the gold can be purified, refined, and made into anything from plates to jewelry.

From Pebbles to Rocks ▶

Rock is a solid material that makes up the earth's crust—the layer of earth just beneath the soil. Rocks are made of one or more minerals, which are natural chemical substances. There are many kinds of rocks, and they come in all shapes and sizes, from tiny pebbles to giant volcanic rocks, like the Devil's Tower, in Wyoming.

Almost as Good as Gold

There is far more silver in the world, so it has never been as valuable as gold. It is also very soft. Silver is so soft that it could never stand the wear and tear of being used as a knife or fork or coin without having other metals added to it to make it sturdy and strong.

Nothing Sparkles Like a Diamond ▲

Both coal and diamonds are formed from carbon. Diamonds, however, are the result of great pressure, which has turned them into pure carbon of amazing clearness and hardness. Diamonds are the hardest known substance on earth, and they are able to cut through any other rock or substance.

A Real Jewel  ▼

Jewels are nothing more than rocks that people have decided are particularly beautiful. Because they are rock, they tend to last a long time, which makes them even more valuable.

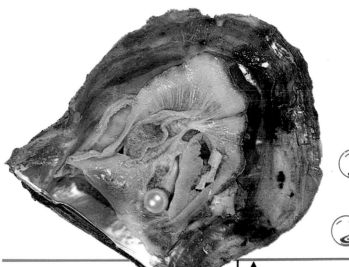

▲ Pearls of Nature

Pearls are not jewels. They are formed around an irritation in an oyster, such as a grain of sand. This grain of sand or dirt inside the oyster's shell slowly becomes covered with a pearl sac. Then nacre, or mother of pearl, is gradually layered onto it. In time, a pearl forms.

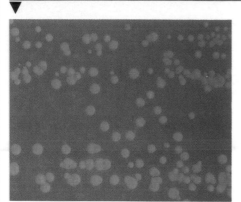

A bacterial culture

Life in Miniature

Bacteria are living things so tiny that they can only be seen with the help of a powerful microscope. They were discovered in the 1600s, when lenses and microscopes were first being developed. Since then, scientists have worked hard to understand these strange living things that are neither plant nor animal but are found everywhere—in the soil, the air, the food we eat, and even the depths of the ocean.

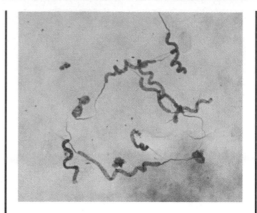

Bacteria News

Bacteria come in all shapes and sizes—although most are colorless. Many are shaped like rods, balls, or corkscrews. Some link together in a chain; others look like a bunch of grapes. There are also bacteria that have tiny hairs on them, which they wave around in order to move from place to place.

Dangerous Bacteria

Typhoid fever, tuberculosis, pneumonia, and even leprosy are all caused by bacteria.

Using Bacteria

There are bacteria that are not harmful at all. Bacteria, for example, cause the decay, or rotting, of dead plants and animals. This breaks down the plant or animal parts into simple substances that, in turn, are used to create new living things. Bacteria also help us make useful items—from leather and cloth to cheese and tea. They are also used to create vaccines, drugs, and other chemicals.

Fruits and Vegetables

A vegetable is just about any plant that you can eat, and the term includes everything from corn to carrots. Fruit is the ovary of a plant—part of its reproductive system that contains seeds. Despite this scientific distinction, we often use the terms incorrectly. Peas, for example, are actually fruit, as are beans and tomatoes.

Eat Your Vegetables! ▲

Vegetables are among the most healthy things you can eat. They contain a wealth of minerals (especially iron and calcium) and vitamins (especially Vitamin A and Vitamin C). Vegetables are also rich in carbohydrates, fats, and proteins. They also provide roughage, the bulk that helps digestive juices work.

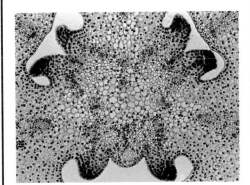

Cell Life ▲

Plants are made up of cells, which are the tiny units from which all life is made. Most plants contain hundreds or even millions of cells, each of which has its own particular job or function to do for the plant to stay alive.

Carrots and Your Eyes

Carrots are rich in *carotene,* a substance that gives them their orange color. Carotene is also rich in Vitamin A, which helps your skin, teeth, and bones. People who do not have enough Vitamin A in their bodies often have "night blindness"—they cannot see in dim light or in the dark. Eating Vitamin-A rich carrots is one way to add carotene to your system and improve your night vision.

◄ Living Things of All Sizes

Plants are one of the two great groups of living things. (The other group, of course, is animals.) They come in all sizes, ranging from one cell all the way up to the largest living things on earth, the giant redwoods (also called sequoias) of California.

The Smallest Living Things

Viruses are the smallest and simplest living things that we have yet discovered. They are so small that if you put one or two million of them side by side they would measure less than half an inch (1 cm).

Plants We Use

Plants are useful to people in many ways. They provide us with the oxygen we breathe. Without them, there probably would not be any life on earth. They provide us with food and clothing and can even be turned into homes. Medicines are also made from many plants.

Plant Production

Scientists experiment with plants in order to have them grow in certain kinds of soil or weather, have more vitamins or minerals, or be better able to stay fresh in your refrigerator. Scientists, for example, have worked to produce new kinds of wheat that have larger grains, more grains, and more food value. These new kinds of wheat even have stronger stems so the plants won't blow down so easily in the wind or rain.

These logs may have ended up as the paper this book is printed on.

Problem Plants

Not all plants are useful. Some plants, like dandelions, ruin people's lawns. Pollen from certain plants causes many people problems with allergies. Other plants attack crops and cost farmers millions of dollars each year. Overgrown plants, like algae and other water-growing plants, can choke out our lakes, rivers, and streams.

The Oldest Living Plant

The bristlecone pine tree in California is probably the oldest living plant on earth. It is between 4,000 and 5,000 years old.

◄ Making New Flowers

A flower—which can be anything from an acorn to a lovely orchid blossom—is the part of a plant that makes the seeds that will someday become a new plant.

The Breath of Life

Photosynthesis is the process by which plants turn the energy of the sun into chemical energy. Plants carry out photosynthesis in order to make their food. This process has an important side effect: As it makes its needed chemical energy, the plant also produces oxygen, which it gives off through its leaves for people and animals to breathe. After people and animals breathe and take in the oxygen they need, they breathe out carbon dioxide gas—which is what plants need to take in to carry out photosynthesis. This exchange between plants and animals helps keep all living things alive on our planet.

Practical Flowers

Flowers are useful—they are not only pretty. For one thing, many of them are used in medicines. Others are used to make perfumes, skin conditioners, and even shampoos. They are especially useful because they help plants reproduce.

Crossbreeding Plants

New kinds of plants are created through "crossbreeding." By finding a wild plant with a certain characteristic that they want to add to another plant, scientists carefully exchange pollen so that the plants will reproduce. Over time—and after generation after generation of plants—scientists can create new plants with the qualities they want.

Bees to Honey ▲

Bees love nectar, a sweet liquid found in many flowers, which they use to make honey. When a bee sees a flower, it will almost always stop to check and see if there is any nectar inside. This process helps both the bee and the plant. When a bee crawls inside a flower, pollen dust falls on it. When it flies off, a bee carries the dust with it until it falls off inside another plant. Spreading pollen this way helps plants reproduce.

The Largest Plants on Earth

Sequoias (also called redwoods) are the world's biggest trees, in part because they are so large in diameter. "General Sherman," the largest sequoia, stands 272 feet (83 m) tall and has a diameter of more than 30 feet (9 m). Mountain ash and Douglas fir trees actually grow taller, even though they are smaller around. The tallest of these trees have reached 330 feet (100 m) in height.

A Few Treeless Spots

Trees of one kind or another will grow just about anywhere. The only parts of the world without them are the Arctic, the Antarctic, and a few desert areas.

Hearty Eaters

Most meat-eating plants can manage to survive without the insects or small animals they catch, even though they are much healthier if their diet includes them. Strangely enough, these plants do not suffer if they "overeat." One poisonous plant, the pitcher plant, has been known to eat as many as 73 cockroaches in two weeks.

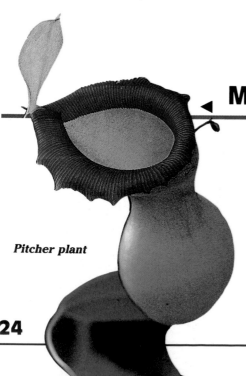

Pitcher plant

Meat-eating Plants

There are over 500 different plants that eat meat of one kind or another. Most of them catch insects or tiny animals for their food. Bacteria and chemicals inside the plant help it to get the nutrients out of its victim.

Two Ways to Shed Leaves

Unlike *deciduous* trees, which shed their leaves every winter, evergreens keep their leaves (or needles) all year long. They lose their leaves little by little all the time. This allows them to grow new, fresh leaves whenever they need them and still stay green all year long.

Saving the Forests

Forests are important because trees, like other green plants, carry out photosynthesis. The oxygen they make is an important part of our world. It is so important, in fact, that if our forests were destroyed, we probably would not be able to survive. For this reason, so many people are concerned that our forests are being cut down all over the world.

Enticing Plants

Pitcher plants are tropical plants that are shaped like a large jug or "pitcher." When insects come close, they get interested in the plant's bright colors and by the sweet-smelling liquid inside the jug. They hurry to the edge of the pitcher to see what is inside—and fall down into the liquid and drown. Once the victim is inside, the plant uses its special chemicals to absorb the insect. Some insects, including some types of flies and mosquitoes, can live inside the pitcher plant's trap with no trouble.

Plants to Drive You Crazy

Locoweed (whose name comes from *loco,* the Spanish word for "crazy") grows in the Midwest and Southwest, and it really is dangerous to horses and cattle. When an animal eats locoweed while grazing, it loses control of its movements and runs around wildly.

The Most Famous Meat-eater

The Venus flytrap, which grows only in North and South Carolina, is the most famous meat-eating plant of all. When it is "hungry," its leaves divide into halves that are hinged together like sections of a book. In the middle of each leaf are three hairs, which are sensitive to the slightest touch. When a fly or other insect sets down on one of these leaves, the two halves snap shut, trapping the insect inside. Ten days later, the insect is gone; it has been "eaten" by the plant.

The stems and leaves of potato plants are poisonous.

Plants to Avoid

There are more than 700 kinds of poisonous plants growing in the United States and Canada alone. Many of them look or smell so nasty that people keep away from them without even thinking. Many plants that we see all the time, or even eat certain parts of, are actually poisonous. Did you know, for example, that the leaves of potato plants and apricot and cherry pits are poisonous? Many poisonous plants harm people and animals if they are eaten. Others cause skin problems or harm the eyes or ears. Some cause problems only to people who are allergic to them.

From Poison to Medicine

A Deadly Poison

DDT, introduced in the 1930s, was a well-known pesticide that was used worldwide. It was especially useful in getting rid of mosquitoes, which spread many diseases in tropical and swampy areas. However, it was found that DDT poisoned birds and fish as well as rivers and lakes. Insects also gradually became immune to the effects of DDT, so that it became less and less useful. In the 1970s, it was taken off the market in most countries.

People have found that some poisonous plants can be turned into medicines. The foxglove plant, for example, can be quite poisonous, but it can also be turned into the medicine digitalis, which is given to people with heart trouble. In the same way, controlled doses of aconite (sometimes called "monkshood"), morphine, quinine, and even strychnine can be used as medicines.

Identifying Plants

The only way to tell if a plant is poisonous is to identify it. You have to look at the plant (or at least pictures of it) and learn what it is and what it does. Do not eat any plant that you do not know about until you check it out.

Traveling Weeds

Weeds get from place to place by the wind or by people or animals. They can even attach themselves to other plants that people actually want. When those plants are put into the earth, the weeds are planted right along with them.

Good Riddance

Weeds are wild plants that grow where they are not wanted. They are extremely tough and hardy, making them almost impossible to get rid of. The most common weeds in the United States are thistles, ragweed, and crabgrass. They cause problems for other plants because they draw food and energy away from them. Weeds also crowd out other plants and spread disease.

Beware of the Weeds!

Certain weeds are really dangerous. In Australia, for example, two different kinds of wild tulips were brought in from South Africa. They have taken over thousands of acres of pastureland, crowding out all the other plants and grasses that could be grown instead. They are also poisonous, so animals (especially cattle) must be kept away from these wild tulips at all times.

Dangerous Pests and Pesticides

For many years, people used pesticides, or chemicals that destroy pests, to help them get rid of unwanted insects that destroyed crops, made recreation areas unpleasant, and caused damage to homes and other buildings. Scientists soon discovered that these chemical pesticides were causing a great deal of damage to our environment—perhaps more harm than they were worth. They entered fruits and vegetables, spreading poisons to birds, animals, fish, and even people. Today, scientists and concerned people are trying to find other ways to get rid of pests.

Getting Rid of Weeds ▲

There are several ways to get rid of weeds. Sometimes, they can be pulled out of the ground. They can also be "starved" by fertilizing the plants you want to grow. As these plants grow and take up more space, they crowd out the weeds. In the past, weed killers were used, but these can also damage good plants as well. Even more importantly, they can cause lasting harm to the soil, allowing terrible poisons to build up in the ground. These poisons can then enter the water supply and reach people and animals. They can also harm other plants— ones that eventually are eaten by people and animals.

Getting Rid of Pests Naturally

"Biological controls" are new, safer ways to control pests such as insects, mice, and rats. Often, one kind of creature is used to get rid of another. Dragonflies, for example, love to eat mosquitoes and gnats. Many governments, therefore, have gone to great lengths to breed and purchase dragonflies so that they can be let loose in areas where people want to get rid of mosquitoes. In the same way, hawks, owls, and other birds of prey can be used to keep down populations of mice and other rodents. Scientists are only beginning to learn about biological controls, but they believe that these controls will help us deal with our environment in a safer, better way in the future.

Pollution Perils ◄

Pollution is anything that poisons the air, water, or land around us. Although there has always been pollution of one kind or another, it clearly is worse—and more dangerous—than ever before. Smoke from factories and cars is one of the main causes of air pollution. Many of the chemicals in this smoke can cause serious health problems. In many cities, these chemicals form *smog,* which is short for "smoke and fog." Smog is a great threat to people who already have problems with their lungs and breathing. It also poisons trees and other plants.

Spreading Acids ▼

Fuels like coal, oil, and gasoline give off acidic fumes when they are burned. Every time the furnace heats your home or you drive in a car, you are sending acids like sulfur dioxide and nitrous dioxide into the atmosphere. These fumes rise up into the air, where they mix with water vapor and form drops of sulfuric acid and nitric acid. These drops fall when it rains, spreading acids all over the planet.

Keeping a Lid on Pollution ▲

Pollution must be controlled, and to do it most of us will have to make changes in how we live. Filters can be used to stop dangerous chemicals from going up into the atmosphere from factories and homes. Cars can be built that burn less fuel and do not cause smog and other problems. Plastic and throw-away containers may have to eliminated in order to prevent the soil from being poisoned. These and other measures will probably have to be taken before the air, water, and soil around us is clean and safe.

Altering Our Climate

The "greenhouse effect" comes from the buildup of carbon dioxide in a layer around the earth as we burn coal, gasoline, and oil. As more and more of these fuels are burned, more and more carbon dioxide is added, trapping the heat of the sun beneath the layer close to the surface of the earth. This "greenhouse effect" (the layer of carbon dioxide is like the glass of a greenhouse, keeping in warm air and stopping cool air from being added) slowly makes the temperature on our planet warmer and warmer. Some scientists believe that the "greenhouse effect" will cause temperatures to rise several degrees in the next 50 years or less. If this happens, weather will change dramatically: Areas where we now grow wheat or corn might suffer from great droughts and the ice at the North and South Poles would begin to melt, causing the sea to rise almost 16 feet (5 m). This could flood many cities and low-lying lands.

Ban that Aerosol Can! ▶

The ozone layer is a region high in our atmosphere in which there is a large amount of the chemical, ozone. Because it is able to absorb ultraviolet light, this layer helps protect the earth from possibly dangerous radiation. It also helps keep the temperature on our planet fairly comfortable most of the time. Unfortunately, air pollution has begun to damage this ozone layer. One of the main offenders is the sprays used in aerosol cans—the cans we use for everything from window cleaner to hair spray. Even though many of these products have been taken off the market, there is still much to do before the ozone layer is safe.

Harmful Acid Rain ▼

Acid rain is harmful to the water in our soil, ponds, and lakes. As trees become more acidic, they become brown and turn sickly, animals cannot find homes or food and disappear, and minerals in the soil wash away. Ponds and lakes become so acidic that nothing— not even the smallest fish or algae plant—can survive in them.

A Lot of Water

Humans have made tremendous demands on the earth's facilities. For example, if all of the fresh water that was diverted from nature for people's use in one year was collected, it would fill a lake the size of Europe with a depth reaching halfway to the earth's core.

From Forest to Desert

The spread of agriculture has had devastating effects, particularly in the poorer parts of the world. Woodlands and scrub are usually invaded by browsing animals such as goats, wood is cut and burned for fuel, and forests are cleared haphazardly for crops. Too often the woodlands and scrub are removed without precautions of terracing and draining channels; the exposed soil is eroded by wind and rain. Erosion now affects two-thirds of the world's nations. In quite a few areas, land has changed from forest to desert within a single generation.

◀ Growing Deserts

In 1985, a government report in Australia warned that two-thirds of the country's tree cover had been destroyed and that more than half of the agricultural land was in need of treatment for erosion. In the Third World, the desert is expanding unchecked. Around the area of the Sahara in Africa, new desert is being created at a rate of 420 acres (170 hectares) an hour.

Lost Species

Scientists believe that at least one unique life form disappears from our planet every day. Many biologists now accept the fact that, unless drastic measures are taken, the earth will have lost between a quarter and a third of all its species of plants and animals by the year 2500.

Threatened Wildernesses

The Arctic and Antarctic are the last two wildernesses of the world that are in danger. These regions are threatened by the lure of wealth. The Antarctic has vast amounts of fish and krill, which is a small shrimplike organism that may someday be exploited as a source of protein. The Arctic, from Alaska through northern Canada and across Siberia, has some of the world's largest deposits of iron, coal, lead, copper, zinc, gold, wolfram, uranium, diamonds, and phosphates, as well as huge untapped reserves of oil and natural gas.

Beautiful National Parks

All over the world, nature reserves and national parks have been developed to protect wildlife and to foster public enjoyment of nature. Yellowstone National Park was the first such park founded in the United States in 1872. The second was the Banff National Park established in Canada in 1885.

Coexisting with Nature

Conservation of nature is the protection of animals and plants in their natural homes. It includes preserving the great variety of species that live on the earth. It also involves the sensible use of all of the earth's resources: its water, soils, minerals, trees, birds, animals, and fish, so that none of them become exhausted and disappear.

Breeding in Captivity

When an animal has become very rare, captive breeding has proved useful to conservationists. The Arabian oryx, the Hawaiian goose, the Puerto Rican parrot, and several other species have been brought back from the verge of extinction by being captured in the wild and bred in zoos. One of the most recent captive breeding programs involves the California condor, which has a wingspan of over 9 feet (3 m). So far, 15 young condors have been hatched in incubators.

Saving the Tropical Forests ▶

In 1985, the World Bank and the World Resources Institute announced their Action Plan for Tropical Forests. The plan includes extensive replanting, aid for poor farmers, and a comprehensive network of large protected areas. Its cost is one billion dollars per year until the end of the 20th century.